JUST FEELINGS

FEELING OF EVERYTHING

DHRUV WAGHELA

Contents

Acknowledgements

I would like to thank everyone who has encouraged me in this journey to fulfill my dream. People who have helped me to achieve my dream of writing my book.

Above all, I'd like to thank my mom who has always loved every sentence I have written without judging me, and also my close friends who have always corrected me.

Thanks to every one of you for always supporting me and it is a privilege to have such amazing people around me Been a wonderful journey, and many more destinies to achieve. JHMH

1. Right Company

I always stay awake at night

But never thought of being alone
Cuz the moon was with me
Cuz air was with me
Cuz night kitlers were with me
Just find the company
Cuz there is always a company

2. Getting a break

• 2 •

Sometimes getting disconnected
And being alone feels good
Cause the mind goes into recovery
But it should not last long
Cause then it goes in depression

3. In The Forest

Being in a forest alone
Is sometimes soothing
We feel fresh and newly
But being a long time alone
Then there comes a fear of
Everything u see in the forest

4. After Ages

• 4 •

After ages seen the rising sun
The mildness and breeze r the same
But the way of perspective has changed
Cause grew a Lil with nature
But not with the world of creature

5. Time Is Relative With Preson

The time which goes in ur day is
It's just not the environment
Its the person with whom u spend ur day
And I got a very happy day
just Day before yesterday

6. You Are Just For Me

The day is good
But nights r not
Cuz ur not there
I feel like ur the energy for me
Ur bright light for me
Ur heartbeat for me
Ur life for me
I feel like ur just for me

7. Never Forget The Driver

V all are waiting for one train

When it arrives we get to our destiny

V all have different destinies

But the trains are same

V follow the path to gain Knowledge to gain experience

But ppl forget to see who runs the train

And never appreciated the driver of the train

8. Perspective

• 8 •

Every living has diff perspective
Which can't be changed
Cause it is their survival
One can't get out of that
Cause they are being molded in that perspective

9. We Never Know The Life

Poverty is not the thing
But compulsion in this world
It's a way to learn In minimal life supply
The way it integrates
Is the way it gets degenerate
Just don't judge too much
Cause it can be ur one of the day

10. Be Happy

To live in a minimalist way
Is the need in life
Cuz it's the way to be happy in life

11. Love is Feeling

Love is subjective
For the ppl in lust
But an emotion
For the ppl who feel
Love is the thing that can be gained
But never be lost
It's in various forms happy or sad
But always love is the feeling not subjective

12. No Need To Prove

The sky is always clear and beautiful
Just clouds make it a bit difficult to see
The sky never tries to prove it is beautiful
Cause it knows that who want to see it beautiful
will be seen by them
In clear and crystal form